Take Heed and Beware of Leaven

Take Heed and Beware of Leaven

Abraham Raymond Eli

Hebron Publishing

Take Heed and Beware of Leaven

By Abraham Raymond Eli

Unless otherwise indicated, all Scripture quotations in this book are from the New King James Version (NKJV) of the Holy Bible. Other versions of the Bible cited in this book are AMP (The Amplified Bible), ERV (Easy-to-Read Version), GNB (The Good News Bible), GW (God's Word), and MSG (The Message Bible)

ISBN 978-978-993-515-4

Cover Photograph: Image by AdrianMedia from Pixabay
(https://pixabay.com/illustrations/preacher-pastor-crooked-dishonest-5331402/)

Cover Design: Hebron Publishing

Contents

Introduction

What did the Lord mean when He said, "take heed and beware"?

*Then Jesus said to them, "Take heed and beware of the leaven of the Pharisees and the Sadducees." (**Matthew 16:6**)*

*Then He charged them, saying, "Take heed, beware of the leaven of the Pharisees and the leaven of Herod." (**Mark 8:15**)*

In the above parallel passages, the Lord Jesus made a declaration to His disciples. This declaration is the subject of this book.

TAKE HEED AND BEWARE

A common thread in these parallel passages is the phrase '*take heed*', and the word '*beware*'. Whenever you come across these terms in Scripture, you need to apply the brakes!

The phrase, '*take heed*', precedes the word, '*beware*'. On its own, *take heed* should get any avid listener to be attentive, as it means, "listen attentively", "pay close attention", or "listen closely" because what is about to follow can save your life! On the other hand, '*beware*' tells us to tread cautiously, to take necessary precautions regarding a matter, and be careful. It is, therefore, a warning!

So, while '*take heed*' gets you to be attentive, '*beware*' brings you a warning. The Amplified Bible translation puts the two terms thus:

> *Be careful and on your guard against (**Matthew 16:6, AMP**)*

> *Look out; keep on your guard and beware (**Mark 8:15, AMP**)*

In **1 Corinthians 10:1-12**, a warning is sounded to all Christians to learn from the errors of Israel in the wilderness. Although Israel was saved from slavery and bondage in Egypt and baptised through the Red Sea crossing, in a figure, yet, many of them did not leave behind the nature of sin associated with the life of bondage to sin and the world, such as rebellion, murmuring, unbelief, etc.

Despite the miracles they witnessed, the spiritual food and drink they enjoyed, the teaching of God's Law by one of the greatest teachers ever, Moses, they still walked contrary to God! As a result, many of them died off in the wilderness and never entered the Promised Land.

The Israelites conducted themselves in a manner that angered God, who is long-suffering and slow to anger! They must have done terrible things to really draw the wrath of God!

When we read about Israel in the wilderness, we are wont to think that they must have been a terrible and ungrateful people. But, writing by the inspiration of the Holy Spirit, Paul, the apostle, warns that the sad epithet of Israel in the wilderness is a warning to us, today's Christians.

Indeed, the world we live in today is our wilderness, as we are on our way to our Promised Land, which is heaven! We have been saved from captivity to sin and the world. We have been saved from God's judgment upon sinners and have been baptised into the Father, the Son, and the Holy Spirit (**Matthew 28:19**). We are being fed with God's word and are partakers of the Holy Spirit. Yet, unless we allow the Holy Spirit to sanctify us, thus empowering us to overcome the lure of sin and the world, we also may not escape the fate that befell Israel in the wilderness.

Therefore, Paul warns,

> *let him who thinks he stands take heed [[**that phrase again**][1] lest he fall. (**1 Corinthians 10:12**)*

The above verse of Scripture is amplified thus:

> *Therefore let anyone who thinks he stands [who feels sure that he has a steadfast mind and is standing firm], take heed lest he fall [into sin]. (**AMP**)*

---

1 Author's infusion

This is a warning to us, today's Christians, not to think of ourselves as invincible and immune to Satan's deception and attack in our self-conceit and self-security.

Indeed, the Bible is replete with similar warnings. Peter, the apostle, warns against being caught off guard by Satan when he wrote by the Holy Spirit:

> *Keep a cool head. Stay alert. The Devil is poised to pounce, and would like nothing better than to catch you napping.* (**1 Peter 5:8, MSG**)

> *But you, friends, are well-warned. Be on guard lest you lose your footing and get swept off your feet by these lawless and loose-talking teachers.* (**2 Peter 3:17, MSG**)

So, when both *"take heed"* and *"beware"* are used in the same sentence, the matter must be of extreme importance. It is the more serious when this warning is coming not just from the early apostles, but more importantly, from the Lord Jesus Christ also!

To put this in a language we would understand, the Lord was saying to His disciples:

"Listen attentively and be on your guard ..."

When you hear such a comment, you should want to know what follows.

PAY CLOSE ATTENTION AND BE CAUTIOUS OF WHAT?

Our Lord Jesus Christ warned His disciples to be cautious of the *leaven* of the Pharisees, Sadducees, and Herodians. In Jesus' day, the Pharisees were religious leaders, the Herodians, politicians, and the Sadducees, a hybrid of both—they were supposed to be spiritual leaders, but in reality, they were politicians using religion as a cloak. So, the Lord warned His disciples to beware of the *leaven* of these religious and political leaders (we will discuss more on these in Chapters 1 and 2).

Let us see the warning in **Mark 8:15** in the Amplified Bible translation:

> *And Jesus [repeatedly and expressly] charged and admonished them, saying, Look out; keep on your guard and beware of the leaven of the Pharisees and the leaven of Herod and the Herodians.* (**AMP**)

The phrase *"repeatedly and expressly"* in the Lord's charge to His disciples in the above **Amplified** translation makes this warning the more crucial. When someone keeps repeating the same message, you will do well to take heed, especially when that 'someone' is Jesus!

The Lord's warning to His disciples at the time is still relevant today, more so, as we see the way the church is being assaulted from within by those who once preached the gospel. The Lord's warning also requires a more in-depth probing concerning what we should pay close attention to and be careful of!

We shall now move on to focus on the subject of *"leaven"*. In Chapter 2, we shall look at the Pharisees, Sadducees, Herodians, and others when we consider purveyors of leaven.

Chapter 1

What is Leaven?

What is the implication of 'leaven' for a Christian?

When Jesus mentioned the word *'leaven'*, His disciples thought He was referring to the bread that people ingest, not just because the people of Jesus' day usually referred to bread as leaven, but more importantly, it was presently the discussion they were engaged in.

> *Now the disciples had forgotten to take bread, and they did not have more than one loaf with them in the boat. Then He charged them, saying, "Take heed, beware of the leaven of the Pharisees and the leaven of Herod." And they reasoned among themselves, saying, "It is because we have no bread." But Jesus, being aware of it, said to them, "Why do you reason because you have no bread? Do you not yet perceive nor understand? Is your heart still hardened? (**Mark 8:14-17**)*

The above passage puts **Mark 8:15** in its proper context. The Lord's response to His disciples' concerns about their thinking regarding bread, makes it essential that we probe the issue of *leaven* further.

WHAT IS LEAVEN?

Leaven is the equivalent of yeast today. It was mixed in the dough to make bread, and its usefulness in bread-making was to make the dough rise before it was put in the oven to bake. So, when the Lord told His disciples to be careful of and watch out for these religious and political leaders' *leaven*, they were confused, and rightly so because they could never fathom the correlation between spiritual and political leaders and bread!

Matthew captures not only the disciples' reaction, which is aptly narrated in **Mark 8:14-17**, but also the clearing up of their misunderstanding by the Lord thus:

> *And they [**Jesus' disciples**][2] reasoned among themselves, saying, "It is because we have taken no bread." But Jesus, being aware of it, said to them, "O you of little faith, why do you reason among yourselves because you have brought no bread? Do you not yet understand, or remember the five loaves of the five thousand and how many baskets you took up? Nor the seven loaves of the four thousand and how many large baskets you took up? How is it you do not understand that I did not speak to you concerning bread? —but to beware of the leaven of the Pharisees and Sadducees." Then they understood that He did not tell them to beware of the leaven of bread, but of the doctrine of the Pharisees and Sadducees. (**Matthew 16:7-12**)*

As the passage reveals, the Lord had to draw His disciples' attention to the miracles of the multiplication of bread to get them to realise that He was not speaking about physical bread, but something more crucial than what was on their minds. The Lord was invariably telling them,

"If I multiplied bread for the multitude, bread should be the last thing on your mind, when I said that you should take heed and beware of the leaven of these religious and political leaders!"[3]

Thus, when the Lord was talking to His disciples about the *leaven* of these religious and political leaders, He used the word '*leaven*' metaphorically.

---

2   Author's infusion

3   Author's paraphrase

LEAVEN AS USED IN SCRIPTURE

In Scripture, generally, *leaven*, besides being regular bread, is a metaphor for a foreign, external, evil, contaminating, or corrupting influence. However, in **Matthew 13:33** and **Luke 13:20-21**, *leaven* is likened to the kingdom of God! This attribution of *leaven* to the kingdom of God creates a problem for us. Does it mean that the kingdom of God is evil? Absolutely not!

There are two schools of thought on the use of *leaven* as an allegory for the kingdom of God: Some say that *leaven* describes a fast, favourable, fascinating, influence of the kingdom of God in the world. Others say that *leaven* represents the crafty, creeping, crawling, contaminating spread of false doctrine, as it corrupts the doctrine of Christ in the hearts of those who lack understanding or spiritual depth! So, while one School of thought sees *leaven* as a positive allegory of God's kingdom in terms of the spread or expanse of the kingdom, another School of thought sees *leaven* as the negative influence of false doctrine on God's kingdom.

However, in the context of **Matthew 16:6** and **Mark 8:15**, which is supported overwhelmingly by other verses of Scripture (**1 Corinthians 5:6; Galatians 5:9**), *leaven* signifies the evil corrupting influence of false doctrine! Here, the term 'doctrine' is broader than teaching, ideology, or philosophy; 'doctrine' is also a way of life and principles for living by such creed.

Leaven is symbolic of sin or anything that corrupts sound biblical doctrine! Any doctrine (including the way of life or manner of living) contrary to Christ's, infuses falsehood into God's word and encourages a lifestyle contrary to Christ and all He stands for, and is, therefore, *leaven*!

In summary, *leaven* refers to the religious and political leaders' doctrine, teaching, ideology, principles, philosophies, politics, way of life, etc., that is apart from Christ and His teaching. Today's disciples of Jesus who are called Christians, would do well to be careful and on guard because strange things are happening in our day that befuddles the mind.

Let us now probe a little deeper into this matter of *leaven*.

THE CHARACTERISTICS OF LEAVEN

Why did the Lord use *leaven* as a metaphor for the religious and political leaders' doctrine and lifestyle? We would be able to understand this as we look at the characteristics of *leaven* and its application to the context of the Lord's statement.

LEAVEN IS FOREIGN TO THE DOUGH AND CHANGES ITS CONSTITUTION

Bread in its purest form is dough without leaven—what is referred to as 'unleavened bread' in Scripture (**Exodus 12:15**). Unleavened bread is flat, dense, and chewy. Only a little is sufficient to satisfy the eater. However, when one adds leaven to dough, it changes the nature of bread. The result is bread that is bloated, lightweight, fluffy, and easier to chew, though not as satisfying as bread without leaven. And it is called leaven—named after the additive—, and rightly so, meaning: leavened, corrupted, impure, or adulterated bread!

Sound doctrine may be hard to digest—comprehend—, especially by the unwilling and unregenerated soul; yet, it is satisfying and filling to those who have been saved and sanctified. Sound doctrine does not excuse sin, but it tells the sinner that there is a way out of sin.

False doctrine—which is symbolised by *leaven*—on the other hand, is lightweight and only campers to the emotions of the listener. It does not warn people against sin; rather, it makes excuses for sin and even encourages sinful conduct by stating that we are under grace and all is forgiven. Some false doctrines even espouse that Jesus' death forgives past, present, and future sins, as though it is a license to sin! Like the leaven of bread, false doctrines adulterate the pure word of God and corrupts the listener, making them lose all inhibitions including, the fear of God!

ONLY A LITTLE LEAVEN IS NEEDED TO SATURATE A WHOLE DOUGH

*A little leaven leavens the whole lump. (**Galatians 5:9**)*

In the above Scripture verse, through Paul, the Holy Spirit was inferring the rabid spread throughout Galatia, of the doctrine of circumcision as the basis for salvation. It is important to note that Galatia was a Roman Province and not a city. So, you can imagine how widespread this false doctrine of circumcision for salvation had spread, shortly after Barnabas and Paul had earlier preached to them, the gospel of salvation by faith alone in Jesus Christ.

Such is the danger of just one false doctrine, that Jesus warned of, and before you know, it will be all over the world in seconds, literally, particularly, with the advent of social media and its accessibility to billions of people around the world!

In another passage of Scripture, the Holy Spirit, again through Paul, refers to the capacity of sin to saturate an entire congregation of believers in Christ if care is not taken thus:

> *Your flip and callous arrogance in these things bothers me* **[referring to the Corinthian Christians' tolerance of sexual immorality, particularly one in which the individual concerned was engaging in it with his stepmother!]**[4]. *You pass it off as a small thing, but it's anything but that. Yeast, too, is a "small thing," but it works its way through a whole batch of bread dough pretty fast. So get rid of this "yeast." Our true identity is flat and plain, not puffed up with the wrong kind of ingredient. The Messiah, our Passover Lamb, has already been sacrificed for the Passover meal, and we are the Unraised Bread part of the Feast.* **(1 Corinthians 5:6-7, MSG)**

Thus, the Holy Spirit is warning that if such despicable conduct were not stamped out, it would soon permeate the entire congregation and even generations to come, as acceptable conduct.

Many unscriptural and abhorrent acts and behaviour have become acceptable in the church of God today in this way. Though such events or behaviour may not have begun with us, but they were passed down from generations past. Not having been stamped out as unacceptable conduct, we now perpetuate it on to the next generation!

One such prominent false doctrine is the celebration of Christmas. This abominable celebration has no Scriptural basis! Nowhere in the Bible did the Lord celebrate His birthday; neither did His disciples after Him nor did He command it! Yet billions of Christians around the world celebrate Christmas as though salvation depended on it! For one, Christmas is built on falsehood, for no one knows the date of Jesus' birth. Secondly, the Lord never instructed the celebration of His birthday! And thirdly, the apostles after Him never once celebrated nor advocated the celebration of the birthday of the Lord.

LEAVEN MAKES THE DOUGH RISE, BUT THE RESULTING BREAD OR LEAVEN IS LESS WEIGHTY

False doctrine gives the impression of a life-transforming message but in actuality, it produces putrefying flatulence and nothing else in the life of its adherents. Hear now what the Lord said:

> *Thus says the LORD of hosts: "Do not listen to the words of the prophets who prophesy to you. They make you worthless; They speak a vision of their own heart, Not from the mouth of the LORD.* **(Jeremiah 23:16)**

---

4   Author's explanation

Indeed, false doctrines make those who follow them feel like they are doing okay spiritually, but they fall apart when adversity arises. False doctrines make people worthless and gives them a false hope! Sadly, several congregations have been established on such falsehood, and ultimately, many will walk into an eternity in hell!

ALTHOUGH LEAVEN TAKES TIME TO FILL THE DOUGH, YET ONCE INTRODUCED, IT SATURATES THE ENTIRE DOUGH

A false doctrine usually starts small—or in a corner—but soon fills Christendom, and before long, it gains prominence and is passed on as *'gospel'*! But hear what Paul said to the Galatians:

> *I am surprised at you! In no time at all you are deserting the one who called you by the grace of Christ, and are accepting another gospel. Actually, there is no "other gospel," but I say this because there are some people who are upsetting you and trying to change the gospel of Christ.* (**Galatians 1:6-7, GNB**)

Paul was disconcerted that the Christians in the region of Galatia had succumbed to the strange doctrine of salvation through circumcision, calling it 'gospel'. As earlier noted in this Chapter, Galatia was a province comprising several cities, towns, and villages, thus emphasising the extent to which false doctrines can spread.

With the advent of the internet and social media, false doctrine travels fast and can fill the entire world in seconds. And once it gets onto the internet highway, it is impossible to retract it. It soon finds its way into the hearts of gullible and impressionable individuals who are not standing firm in their Christian walk! And before long, it takes on a life of its own, and because we live in a time when what the majority are doing is acceptable, virtually everyone gets to imbibe such false doctrine!

THE CONSEQUENCES OF LEAVEN

Under the Old Covenant, God expressly prohibited leaven from being seen in any home throughout the seven days of the Passover (**Exodus 12:15**). God strictly prohibited using leaven in any offering by fire because those offerings were holy (**Leviticus 2:11; 6:17; 10:12**). Thus, the shewbread in the Holy Place was unleavened bread.

And because *leaven* is symbolic of sin, it was prohibited from virtually all sacred offerings, foods, and events. In Israel, this would be essentially all-year-round! Indeed, the use of leaven, where prohibited, was a severe infraction, and God demanded the cutting off of anyone in breach from Israel's commonwealth (**Exodus 12:19**)!

Generally, *leaven*, in Scripture, is anything that corrupts the doctrine of Christ. In effect, *leaven* is emblematic of a false gospel, a message contrary to Christ's, and a lifestyle contrary to what God expects of a Christian.

God reveals the seriousness with which He views the adulteration or corruption of His message thus,

> *For I testify to everyone who hears the words of the prophecy of this book: If anyone adds to these things, God will add to him the plagues that are written in this book; and if anyone takes away from the words of the book of this prophecy, God shall take away his part from the Book of Life, from the holy city, and from the things which are written in this book. (**Revelation 22:18-19**)*

Those who add to God's word, plagues will be added upon them. Those who subtract from it, will have their names removed from the Book of Life, and therefore, an eternity in hell! Thus, the consequences of imbibing and living by false doctrine is an eternity in hell—a cutting-off from the commonwealth or inheritance of the saints of God!

WHAT SHOULD WE DO ABOUT LEAVEN?

Now that we have seen the nature and consequences of *leaven* for the church of God, it is only natural to seek a way of not entangling with it. Below, we proffer such.

AVOID THEM COMPLETELY

In the light of the devastating and sometimes irreversible impact of false doctrine or philosophies and ideologies on those who adhere to them, Christians would do well to avoid altogether, the teachings or philosophies of false prophets or politicians masquerading as religious leaders.

One of the consequences of not avoiding false doctrine but entertaining them, is, syncretism. Syncretism is the practice of the admixture of several beliefs; in which case, this admixture of beliefs effectively ceases to be Christianity! We earlier pointed to the celebration of Christmas, which is one of such syncretic practices. Another is the practice of praying in the name of *"the god of pastor so and so"*.

We have already been told to pray in the name of Jesus. Yet, many pastors gloat over their names being associated with praying to God, as though it is in response to their righteousness that God is answering the prayers of their congregants. What arrogance!

Let me make it as clear as I can that our prayers in Jesus' name is because He alone is acceptable to God as the perfect sacrifice for sin!

Like Paul noted:

> *Christ has been divided into groups! Was it Paul who died on the cross for you? Were you baptised as Paul's disciples?* (**1 Corinthians 1:13, GNB**)

God responds to our prayers because of Jesus Christ not because of some senior pastor, bishop, or even General Overseer. Besides, we do not know the 'god' of many of these pastors!

QUICKLY IDENTIFY AND NEUTRALISE THEM

As leaven in the dough, false doctrine is foreign to—and should never mix with—the doctrine of Christ! It is harmful to the soul. You must, therefore, quickly identify and instantly neutralise it. Identifying false doctrine means that you are a student of the Bible, are open to the teaching of the Holy Spirit, and are yielded to the Holy Spirit's prodding. You must note that the Bible does not lend itself to the private interpretation of any individual.

> *knowing this first, that no prophecy of Scripture is of any private interpretation, for prophecy never came by the will of man, but holy men of God spoke as they were moved by the Holy Spirit.* (**2 Peter 1:20-21**)

The Bible always interprets itself. If you tarry enough in the word of God and prayer and are open to the Holy Spirit, you will obtain the correct interpretation of Scripture.

> *Do your best to win full approval in God's sight, as a worker who is not ashamed of his work, one who correctly teaches the message of God's truth.* (**2 Timothy 2:15, GNB**)

Unfortunately, if any false teaching ever takes root, nothing can be done but to circumvent it. This is an arduous task for a young believer in Christ.

In interpreting **Matthew 13:24-30**, the Parable of the Tares and Wheat, the Lord said,

> *He who sows the good seed is the Son of Man. The field is the world, the good seeds are the sons of the kingdom, but the tares are the sons of the wicked one. The enemy who sowed them is the devil, the harvest is the end of the age, and the reapers are the angels. Therefore as the tares are gathered and burned in the fire, so it will be at the end of this age. The Son of Man will send out His angels, and they will gather out of His kingdom all things that offend, and those who practice lawlessness, and will cast them into the furnace of fire. There will be wailing and gnashing of teeth. Then the righteous will shine forth as the sun in the kingdom of their Father. He who has ears to hear, let him hear! (**Matthew 13:37-43**)*

In this interpretation, the Lord lets us know what happened after Satan sowed evil seeds (false brethren and their doctrine) alongside the Lord's seeds (the children of the kingdom of God and Christ's doctrine). When the servants detected the co-mingling of seeds, the Lord said that they should be left to grow side-by-side; otherwise, in uprooting the evil seeds, some of the good seeds would be destroyed. This means that both sound and false doctrines will have to dwell side-by-side. So, the good seed will have to circumnavigate the world around them to attain eternal life!

Thus, if you are going to minimise having to side-step strange doctrines, you would do well not to entertain them in the first place. Some Christians are curious about wanting to hear something new—like the Athenians on Mars Hill (**Acts 17:16-21**)—and they end up imbibing doctrines that prove stubborn to expunge from their lives. So, it is better to shoot down any doctrine that is contrary to Christ before they take root in your life.

CONTINUALLY FILL YOUR MIND WITH THE WORD OF GOD

Though false doctrines may appear to be harmless and insignificant, yet their impact and spread are devastating! To keep false doctrines out, always fill your mind with the word of God:

> *And do not be conformed to this world, but be transformed by the renewing of your mind, that you may prove what is that good and acceptable and perfect will of God. (**Romans 12:2**)*

Do not allow into your mind, any unscriptural teaching, no matter how well it may sound. Remember that,

> *a little leaven leavens the whole lump (**1 Corinthians 5:6**)*

and indeed, we see even now in our day, entire congregations being contaminated with false doctrines!

Though they may take time to corrupt or contaminate a Christian's walk with God or a local assembly's lifestyle, false doctrines will undoubtedly continue to work therein until they turn the believer or local congregation entirely away from God! Therefore, continually fill your life with the word of God and sound doctrine (**Ephesians 3:17; Colossians 3:16**)! And for the ministers of the gospel,

> *Preach the word! Be ready in season and out of season. Convince, rebuke, exhort, with all long-suffering and teaching. For the time will come when they will not endure sound doctrine, but according to their own desires, because they have itching ears, they will heap up for themselves teachers; and they will turn their ears away from the truth, and be turned aside to fables. (***2 Timothy 4:2-4***)*

If you find that you have the propensity for picking up new revelations, my advice to you is to remember that:

> *All things continue the way they have been since the beginning. The same things will be done that have always been done. There is nothing new in this life. Someone might say, "Look, this is new," but that thing has always been here. It was here before we were. (***Ecclesiastes 1:9-10, ERV***)*

Though it may be new to you, it is not new at all! And if such *'revelation'* is not in the Bible as an express command of God and applicable to the New Testament believer, it must be dismissed offhand! God's word also warns you to

> *Keep your heart with all diligence, For out of it spring the issues of life. (***Proverbs 4:23***)*

Do not be so open to spiritual things that you leave yourself unprotected from foreign and strange doctrines. You must 'install' within you, a 'filtration' mechanism to sieve out anything that is not of God! This mechanism is made possible by being sensitive to the Holy Spirit and His nudgings. The Bible speaks of the *"discerning of spirits"*, one of the spiritual gifts mentioned in **1 Corinthians 12:8-10**. This is one gift we can all do with, lest we allow what should not be allowed into our lives, and disallow what ought to be allowed.

BE WATCHFUL AND PRAYERFUL AT ALL TIMES

The Lord warned us to be observant and prayerful, lest we fall into temptation (**Matthew 26:41**). The devil does not present false doctrine as obviously abhorrent; he makes it sound right and plausible enough for the unsuspecting. If you are not watchful and prayerful, you also can be taken in. Can you imagine how many times you have fallen for Satan's tricks?

Satan's approach is subtle. He lures people with sentiments and statements like, "Everyone is doing it" or "What can be wrong with it?" Once you find yourself trying to rationalise an action, then you are very likely in the grips of Satan and trying to justify an act you know full-well you should not be engaging in.

When you want to make decisions based on evaluation of pros and cons, you are following Satan's direction. With God, it is a command, not a cost-benefit analysis! And it is in the place of prayer that you get to hear God clearly on any matter, so keep praying!

The Lord taught us to pray,

> *". . . do not lead us into temptation, But deliver us from the evil one." (**Matthew 6:13**)*

The Holy Spirit, through Peter, warns us to

> *Be sober, be vigilant; because your adversary the devil walks about like a roaring lion, seeking whom he may devour. Resist him, steadfast in the faith, knowing that the same sufferings are experienced by your brotherhood in the world. (**1 Peter 5:8-9**)*

Indeed, let us do more than just pray. Let us also watch. Be cautious and careful about what is being offered as doctrine. Suppose a doctrine, principle, or philosophy is not based in Scripture? No matter the renown of its author or propagator, such doctrine, principle, or philosophy, must be discarded promptly and decisively—do not give it a second thought!

Chapter 2

The Purveyors of Leaven

Who are the purveyors of leaven? Are they still with us today?

WHO IS A PURVEYOR OF LEAVEN?

A purveyor, in general, is anyone who sells or supplies goods or services. Purveyors of leaven in Israel, would be unable to sell their merchandise to the priests or unleavened bread bakers during the Passover and other religious feasts because the business of leaven would only be profitable to people who care nothing for the observance of the Law.

The natural question would then be, "Why bother to stock leaven?" Well, they would bother as long as there are buyers! So, a purveyor of leaven in Israel was sustained in business by those who bought leaven. If there were no buyers, the industry would naturally die!

We had previously established that biblical *leaven* represents sin, corruption, contamination, etc. Therefore, a purveyor of biblical *leaven* is anyone who promotes anything that corrupts the word of God; for example, giving a wrong interpretation of Scripture, introducing and eliciting unscriptural practices, etc.

Purveyors of biblical *leaven* are those who disseminate and proclaim false doctrines and human philosophies as a substitute for sound biblical doctrine, and rational thinking, instead of promoting or teaching faith in God. These men and women are in 'business', so to speak, because people 'buy' what they are 'peddling'!

Indeed, one would not expect purveyors of *leaven* to be Christians lest they be in danger of being cut off from God! Alas! many purveyors of *leaven* are Christians or were once Christians before going rogue!

In the Gospels and in the Book of Revelation, the Lord Jesus mentioned six purveyors of *leaven*: the Herodians, the Sadducees, the Pharisees, the Nicolaitans, the Balaamites, and the Jezebels. Let us now discuss these purveyors of leaven.

THE HERODIANS

The Herodians were Jewish members of the political ruling class, with affiliation to the Roman Empire. They were irreligious but teamed up with the Pharisees to oppose Jesus (**Mark 3:6; 12:13; Matthew 22:16**). In response to one of the traps they set for Jesus about taxes, the Lord responded with the famous line:

> *"Give to Caesar what belongs to Caesar, and give to God what belongs to God." (**Matthew 22:21, ERV**)*

The Herodians cared nothing about religion, they just did not want some 'fanatic' religious 'neophyte' like Jesus coming to upset the peace and status quo they were enjoying. And once the Pharisees and Sadducees did not agree with Jesus' teachings, they lent their political weight to take Him out of the way!

THE SADDUCEES

The Sadducees were mostly priests who constituted the majority in the Sanhedrin which was the religious Council of the day (**Acts 5:17**), though a few of them were wealthy businessmen. They denied the resurrection of the dead; they did not believe in angels and spirits (**Matthew 22:23; Acts 23:8**), and by implication, did not also believe in heaven and hell nor eternal judgment! And to think that these were supposedly the custodians of the Mosaic Law!

The Sadducees erred scripturally, not knowing the scriptures nor the power of God (**Matthew 22:23-32**). They ridiculed the resurrection of the dead which they did not believe and sneered at the suggestion that there is life after death. Their influence had waned from way back Old Testament times (**1 Samuel 2:12-17; Jeremiah 5:30-31**), and in Jesus' day, they were barely hanging on because of the overbearing influence of the Pharisees. They were thus unwilling to allow a 'nobody' like Jesus, with no known affiliation to any of the Scribes or Rabbis come and further erode their already battered image.

The Sadducees were doctrinally at odds with the Pharisees but colluded with them to oppose Jesus and His doctrine (**John 11:47-50**)!

THE PHARISEES

The Pharisees were not priests but ordinary citizens who sought to maintain religious purity among the Jews by ensuring strict observance of Mosaic laws. However, they added to the Law, the *'traditions of the elders'* (**Matthew 15:3**) and trumped them over Mosaic Law. Paul seemed to have inferred this when he wrote:

> *They have not known the way in which God puts people right with himself, and instead, they have tried to set up their own way; and so they did not submit themselves to God's way of putting people right. (**Romans 10:3, GNB**)*

The Lord Jesus recognised them as those who occupied Moses' seat, thus, acknowledging their role as the real custodians of Mosaic Law. Therefore, Jesus asked the people to give heed to their teaching of the Law. He, however, warned them not to imitate their lifestyle because of their hypocrisy (we will discuss this in detail in Chapter 3).

The problem of the Pharisees in their role can be summed up in two statements made by the Lord. The first is in **Matthew 9:12-13** and the second, in **Matthew 23:2-7**.

> [10]*Now it happened, as Jesus sat at the table in the house, that behold, many tax collectors and sinners came and sat down with Him and His disciples.* [11]*And when the Pharisees saw it, they said to His disciples, "Why does your Teacher eat with tax collectors and sinners?"* [12]*When Jesus heard that, He said to them, "Those who are well have*

> *no need of a physician, but those who are sick. ¹³But go and learn what this means: 'I desire mercy and not sacrifice.' For I did not come to call the righteous, but sinners, to repentance." (**Matthew 9:10-13**)*

The application of the law by the Pharisees lacked compassion, particularly, on the less privileged and thus oppressed the already down-trodden. The Pharisees had suddenly become elitist and unfeeling of the grief of the poor and commoners, of which they once were.

> *²"The scribes and the Pharisees sit in Moses' seat. ³Therefore whatever they tell you to observe, that observe and do, but do not do according to their works; for they say, and do not do. ⁴For they bind heavy burdens, hard to bear, and lay them on men's shoulders; but they themselves will not move them with one of their fingers. ⁵But all their works they do to be seen by men. They make their phylacteries broad and enlarge the borders of their garments. ⁶They love the best places at feasts, the best seats in the synagogues, ⁷greetings in the marketplaces, and to be called by men, 'Rabbi, Rabbi.' (**Matthew 23:2-7**)*

The Pharisees had carved out a sacred place for themselves and were no longer interested in God. They only cared for the privileges associated with being praised and revered in public by the citizenry. They enacted rules which they could not keep, but insisted that others kept them.

Their hypocrisy was a mark of their lifestyle; thus, the Lord pronounced woes upon them. They teamed up with the Herodians and Sadducees—talk of strange bed-fellows—to oppose and eliminate Jesus. Not only did the Pharisees not understand the full implications of the Law, they also did not have the Spirit of God in them to direct and reveal to them who Jesus was. They coldly implemented the Law until it concerned them:

> *Now He was teaching in one of the synagogues on the Sabbath. And behold, there was a woman who had a spirit of infirmity eighteen years, and was bent over and could in no way raise herself up. But when Jesus saw her, He called her to Him and said to her, "Woman, you are loosed from your infirmity." And He laid His hands on her, and immediately she was made straight, and glorified God. But the ruler of the synagogue answered with indignation, because Jesus had healed on the Sabbath; and he said to the crowd, "There are six days on which men ought to work; therefore come and be healed on them, and not on the Sabbath day." The Lord then answered him and said, "Hypocrite! Does not each one of you on the Sabbath*

*loose his ox or donkey from the stall, and lead it away to water it? So ought not this woman, being a daughter of Abraham, whom Satan has bound—think of it—for eighteen years, be loosed from this bond on the Sabbath?" (**Luke 13:10-16**)*

Like the Lord noted in the above Scripture passage, the same Pharisees who would not care for the healing of an infirmed person on a Sabbath, permitted their livestock to drink and graze on a Sabbath. The Law of the Sabbath forbade their livestock to graze, but to rest also.

THE NICOLAITANS

We do not know much about the Nicolaitans except that the Lord hated their teaching and lifestyle (**Revelation 2:6, 15**). Going by **Revelation 2:14-15**, the Nicolaitans were propagating the doctrine of Balaam, which encouraged licentiousness with sacred things. In fact, the **Living Bible** translation refers to them as *"followers of Balaam"* with a footnote explanation: *"Nicolaitans, which, when translated from Greek to Hebrew, becomes Balaamites, who were followers of the man who induced the Israelites to fall by lust. (see [Revelation][5] 2:14 and Numbers 31:15-16.)"*[6]

Thus, we can say that any doctrine or lifestyle that encourages moral looseness qualifies as the Nicolaitans' doctrine and is utterly abhorred by the Lord.

THE BALAAMITES

The Balaamites propagate the doctrine of Balaam, which entails idolatry, profiting from the gospel (**2 Peter 2:15; Jude 1:11**), and practicing sexual immorality (**Revelation 2:14**). Their trademark is the *'prosperity gospel'* and unbridled freedom manifesting as sensuality.

Balaam is the prophet to whom this group was affiliated. When Balaam saw that he was not going to get paid by Balak, he advised Balak to release the Midianite women into Israel's camp to seduce them into sexual immorality and idolatry. Balaam knew that by so doing, God would be angry with Isreal and kill them Himself.

---

5   Authors infusion to make Scripture citation relevant.

6   The Living Bible (1971), Tyndale House Publishers, Inc. Carol Stream, Illinois 60188. pp 1047

Like their patriarch, Balaamites do not care about the consequence of their doctrine, so long as it brings them profit. They would say and do anything for profit (**Jude 1:11**)! They do not care that what they are doing will lead men astray and away from God!

THE JEZEBELS

In His message to the church in Thyatira, the Lord said a self-styled prophetess, Jezebel, taught and seduced the church into sensuality, adultery, idolatry, and the occult (**Revelation 2:20-24**). The Lord named this woman after King Ahab's wife. We can thus, infer that both Jezebels were of the same spirit!

King Ahab's Gentile, idolatrous wife, Jezebel, influenced an already wicked Ahab to become exceedingly evil, supervised the slaughter of God's children, and was herself a seductress—the epitome of evil (**1 Kings 16:31; 18:4; 21:25; 2 Kings 9:22, 30**).

Thus, some of the traits of Jezebels are manipulating church leaders and leadership to do evil, supervising the destruction of the righteous and the practice of unrighteousness, seducing God's children to practice sensuality and sexual immorality, and to engage in idolatry and occultic practices (**1 Kings 16:31; 18:4; 21:1-16, 25; 2 Kings 9:22, 30**). Jezebels have the pastor's ear, who also allows them to teach the church.

Ahab's children by Jezebel were themselves wicked. Through the marriage of Jehoshaphat's son to Athaliah, Ahab's daughter, Ahab (an extremely wicked king) and Jehoshaphat (a righteous king) became allies. It was an unholy alliance that almost cost Jehoshaphat his life. The marriage between Jehoshaphat's son and Jezebel's daughter almost resulted in the entire nation becoming a demonic enclave, because of Athaliah's influence and her attempt to usurp the throne in the kingdom of Judah.

In the Book of Revelation, the Jezebel mentioned therein had daughters or what we may call, protégés or followers, who negatively influenced the church to engage in evil, just like Athaliah did to her husband, son, and very nearly the whole of the nation of Judah.

One very crucial thing to note about Jezebels and their protégés is that, they are never repentant! The Lord said that He had given the Jezebel in the Book of Revelation and her protégés time to repent, but like Ahab's Jezebel, they too refused to repent of their evil deeds.

TODAY'S PURVEYORS OF LEAVEN

The purveyors of *leaven* in Jesus' day and Asia Minor (which was the location of the seven churches of the Book of Revelation) have died. Still, their philosophies and practices continue to date! In the place of the First Century purveyors of *leaven*, we now have daring men and women of renown, who brazenly and freely teach their destructive and heretic messages which are alien to Scripture.

Today, in every nation where Christianity is widely accepted, we have politicians or the ruling class who, though irreligious, would claim to be Christians for votes! They would team up with any religious group, regardless of their beliefs, provided such an alliance would help to advance their political career.

These elected officials and their appointees attend church services mostly for optics. They know nothing of, and neither care anything for God. They are quick to call for prayers when things fall apart. Yet, their wickedness manifests in the discharge of their duties. They engage in graft, promote corruption, thuggery, conspiracy theories, and harassment of political opponents. They are unconcerned for the poor and the socially disadvantaged.

Then, there are the renowned religious leaders and scholars whose secular opinions or views and disposition oppose God's word. Such opposition is always glaring when God's word in interpretation contradicts their thinking! These are leaders and scholars who have elevated their church doctrine above the doctrine of Christ. These spiritual leaders are double-faced; teaching one thing but secretly living a completely untoward lifestyle.

Also, there are the Jezebels—the seducers and seductresses—, and those who operate cults in the church. These are not outsiders but people who are within the church. They preach sensuality and live sensually, subverting whole congregations to follow their adulterous and occultic ways. They are unrepentant in all they do and can be of either gender.

Modern-day purveyors of false doctrines teach freedom without boundaries and freely dispense their strange teachings, encouraging their congregants to live as they choose, without any thought for dire consequences. The fear of God does not attend their preaching. Their interest is in their members attending their programmes. They pay little or no attention to the transformation of the congregants by the Holy Spirit's power.

Today's purveyors of *leaven* are always talking about money, fame, pleasure, and the world leaders that they have recently visited. They use the name of Jesus to deceive the unsuspecting and engage in lying wonders which they call 'miracles'. They prophesy and propagate a distorted message, for which there is no corroboration in Scripture! They preach a prosperity message that feeds their ostentation and breeds selfishness and avarice in their adherents. Below is God's judgment on these individuals:

> *The LORD Almighty said to the people of Jerusalem, "Do not listen to what the prophets say; they are filling you with false hopes. They tell you what they have imagined and not what I have said. To the people who refuse to listen to what I have said, they keep saying that all will go well with them. And they tell everyone who is stubborn that disaster will never touch them." I said, "None of these prophets has ever known the LORD's secret thoughts. None of them has ever heard or understood his message, or ever listened or paid attention to what he said. His anger is a storm, a furious wind that will rage over the heads of the wicked, and it will not end until he has done everything he intends to do. In days to come his people will understand this clearly." The LORD said, "I did not send these prophets, but even so they went. I did not give them any message, but still they spoke in my name. If they had known my secret thoughts, then they could have proclaimed my message to my people and could have made them give up the evil lives they live and the wicked things they do. (Jeremiah 23:16-22, GNB)*

HOW SHOULD WE RESPOND TO PURVEYORS OF LEAVEN?

The appropriate response to these *'leaven merchants'* is, first, identify them, then avoid them! Also, do not encourage them but contend earnestly for the faith! Let us now expound on these responses.

IDENTIFYING PURVEYORS OF LEAVEN

By their character and conduct, purveyors of *leaven* can be identified.

> *You will know them by their fruits. (Matthew 7:16)*

True Christians manifest the *fruit of the Spirit* or the divine nature, which is the nature of God; whereas, purveyors of *leaven* exhibit the works of the flesh or the wrong actions of the sinful human nature. So, when the Lord spoke in **Matthew 7:16**, He was challenging us to test for fruit in people who come to us in His name. In **Galatians 5**, we see the difference between the *fruit of the Spirit* and the works of the flesh.

> *Now the works of the flesh are evident, which are: adultery, fornication, uncleanness, lewdness, idolatry, sorcery, hatred, contentions, jealousies, outbursts of wrath, selfish ambitions, dissensions, heresies, envy, murders, drunkenness, revelries, and the like; of which I tell you beforehand, just as I also told you in time past, that those who practice such things will not inherit the kingdom of God. But the fruit of the Spirit is love, joy, peace, longsuffering, kindness, goodness, faithfulness, gentleness, self-control. (**Galatians 5:19-23**)*

Any fruit apart from the *fruit of the Spirit* is not of God! It is of human or satanic origin. And anyone manifesting any trait that is not of God, yet preaching the gospel, is a purveyor of *leaven*.

Purveyors of *leaven* may be hard to identify by mere observation, especially when you have not spent appreciable time with them. But through the Holy Spirit, they are revealed through spiritual discernment and prayer. When you ask God in prayer, He will tell you who is authentic and who is not.

Jude notes that they sneak into the church undetected:

> *What has happened is that some people have infiltrated our ranks (our Scriptures warned us this would happen), who beneath their pious skin are shameless scoundrels. Their design is to replace the sheer grace of our God with sheer license—which means doing away with Jesus Christ, our one and only Master. (**Jude 1:4, MSG**)*

and Paul warns that,

> *They'll make a show of religion, but behind the scenes they're animals. ... [**they**][7] ... smooth-talk themselves into the homes of unstable and needy women and take advantage of them; women who, depressed by their sinfulness, take up with every new religious fad that calls itself "truth." (**2 Timothy 3:5-6, MSG**)*

They are Satan's ministers transforming themselves into ministers of righteousness (**2 Corinthians 11:13-15**). Peter tells us that,

> *They're only out for themselves. They'll say anything, anything, that sounds good to exploit you. (**2 Peter 2:3, MSG**)*

So, beware of smooth-talking 'evangelists' and oratorial speakers peddling a strange message which they term 'revelation', 'proph-

---

7   Author's infusion

ecy', or 'gospel'! The messages they proclaim are generally incongruent with the word of God and oppose the truth that is in God's word. Sometimes it may seem that they are saying the truth, but their unscriptural inferences and conclusions expose the falsehood in their statements.

If you wait patiently, you will soon see the cracks in the veneer they have pasted over their untoward character. The human and satanic nature would, sooner than you can imagine, show up. Like the Yorubas in Nigeria say,

"Human nature is like smoke; it cannot be covered for long"!

So, never get comfortable with anyone whose pedigree you know nothing of and whose *fruit* you have not subjected to the test!

> *My dear friends, don't believe everything you hear. Carefully weigh and examine what people tell you. Not everyone who talks about God comes from God. There are a lot of lying preachers loose in the world. Here's how you test for the genuine Spirit of God. Everyone who confesses openly his faith in Jesus Christ—the Son of God, who came as an actual flesh-and-blood person—comes from God and belongs to God. And everyone who refuses to confess faith in Jesus has nothing in common with God. This is the spirit of antichrist that you heard was coming. Well, here it is, sooner than we thought! My dear children, you come from God and belong to God. You have already won a big victory over those false teachers, for the Spirit in you is far stronger than anything in the world. These people belong to the Christ-denying world. They talk the world's language and the world eats it up. (**1 John 4:1-5, MSG**)*

AVOID THEM AND THEIR MESSAGES

Do not try to engage purveyors of *leaven*; rather, avoid them like the plague. More importantly, shun their messages! They can be persuasive and have subverted whole households (**Titus 1:11**) and led many unsuspecting people astray (**2 Timothy 3:6-7**). Scripture warns us to,

> *Stay clear of these people. (**2 Timothy 3:5, MSG**)*

Their messages are everywhere—television, internet, social media, etc.—encouraging avarice, civil disobedience, pleasure, etc.

> *Don't be naive. There are difficult times ahead. As the end approaches, people are going to be self-absorbed, money-hungry, self-promoting, stuck-up, profane, contemptuous*

> *of parents, crude, coarse, dog-eat-dog, unbending, slanderers, impulsively wild, savage, cynical, treacherous, ruthless, bloated windbags, addicted to lust, and allergic to God. They'll make a show of religion, but behind the scenes they're animals. Stay clear of these people. These are the kind of people who smooth-talk themselves into the homes of unstable and needy women and take advantage of them; women who, depressed by their sinfulness, take up with every new religious fad that calls itself "truth." They get exploited every time and never really learn. (2 Timothy 3:1-7, MSG)*

Modern purveyors of *leaven* are ever ready to prophesy and would send you something in return for a donation! They are those who ask you to give money to God for a healing or miracle, yet the Lord Jesus said,

> *Heal the sick, bring the dead back to life, heal those who suffer from dreaded skin diseases, and drive out demons. You have received without paying, so give without being paid. (Matthew 10:8, GNB)*

Do not let curiosity get the better of you — change the channel, scroll away, or switch to something edifying. Remember,

> *"A little leaven leavens the whole lump" (Galatians 5:9)*

DO NOT ENCOURAGE THEM

John, the Elder, warns:

> *Anyone who gets so progressive in his thinking that he walks out on the teaching of Christ, walks out on God. ... If anyone shows up who doesn't hold to [the][8] ... teaching [of Christ][9], don't invite him in and give him the run of the place. That would just give him a platform to perpetuate his evil ways, making you his partner. (2 John 1:9-11, MSG)*

By donating to and accommodating purveyors of *leaven* and their cause, you are invariably encouraging them, and unfortunately, partaking in their sins!

> *If a person is involved in some serious sins, you don't want to become an unwitting accomplice. (1 Timothy 5:22, MSG)*

---

8   Author's infusion

9   Author's infusion

When you support purveyors of *leaven*, you encourage them to engage in their perversion continually. Therefore, do not encourage them!

CONTEND EARNESTLY FOR THE FAITH

It is not enough to avoid *'leaven merchants'* and their messages; we must also propagate the true gospel. John Stuart Mill (1867) is attributed with the saying:

"Bad men need nothing more to compass their ends, than that good men should look on and do nothing."[10]

If we do not spread the authentic gospel and teach the true and unadulterated doctrine of Christ, *leaven* will soon fill the airwaves! Thus Jude charged:

> *Dear friends, I wanted very much to write to you about the salvation we all share together. But I felt the need to write to you about something else: I want to encourage you to fight hard for the faith that God gave his holy people. God gave this faith once, and it is good for all time.* (*Jude 1:3, ERV*)

It is incumbent on us, who know and have the truth, to vigorously and earnestly get the glorious message of Christ out to the world through television, the internet, social media, etc. We cannot afford to play the ostrich while the world, and even the church, is being filled with *leaven*.

Today, sadly, Christianity is perceived as tolerant of licentiousness, crass materialism, sensuality, and corruption. It is seen as supporting evil which is incongruent with the doctrine of Christ. Like the Sadducees, some church leaders are only about political power and the misuse of Scripture for selfish and self-seeking purposes. They are quiet most of the time until election season when they begin to prophesy about who will win the elections—false prophesies, more like predictions—in the hope of being a part of the emergent political power!

We must change the narrative. We must not leave the communication space to people who do not have the truth that changes lives. Let us brace up and contend for the faith which was handed to us by the Lord Himself! Like Jude, let us drop everything and put forth the truth of Christ as contained in Scripture—put it out there! People may not heed the truth today, but someday or in some other generation, they would. Today, we benefit from the Early Chris-

---

10   "The Top 10: Misattributed Quotations" in The Independent (https://www.independent.co.uk/voices/top-10-misattributed-quotations-a7910361.html)

tians' works; tomorrow's Christians could profit from ours.

GOD'S WARNING AGAINST PURVEYORS OF LEAVEN IS STILL RELEVANT TODAY

The '*leaven merchants*' divide the church along denominational lines, such as Charismatic, Pentecostal, Baptist, Catholic, etc. and, along racial and ethnic lines such as White Evangelicals, African American churches, indigenous churches, etc. But the Bible says, there is neither Jew nor Greek; rich nor poor; Caucasian nor Negroid nor Mongoloid in Christendom. These divisions are the purveyors' methods to gain an inroad into people's hearts and hard-earned cash. The church must unite around Christ, not around men and women—even if they are church leaders!

The Lord warned His disciples about the purveyors of leaven of His day. He warned those in Asia Minor through John, the Elder, about the purveyors of *leaven* of their day. Now He is warning us against heeding the sales pitches of the purveyors of *leaven* of our day. Beware! These slick individuals are selling poison!

Chapter 3

The Leaven of Hypocrisy

How is leaven hypocrisy? Is hypocrisy in the church today?

LEAVEN AND YOUR LIFESTYLE

*He [**Jesus**][11] began to say to His disciples first of all, "Beware of the leaven of the Pharisees, which is hypocrisy." (Luke 12:1)*

Let me emphasise that *leaven* depicts more than what is spoken or written; it conveys the meaning both of speech and conduct because of its propensity to corrupt a person's way of life.

---

11   Author's clarification

The Bible says,

> *But don't fool yourselves. Don't let yourselves be poisoned by this anti-resurrection loose talk. "Bad company ruins good manners." (**1 Corinthians 15:33, MSG**)*

Purveyors of *leaven* corrupt, infect, and negatively influence others by their talk and lifestyle. So, when the Lord warned His disciples to,

> *"Beware of the leaven of the Pharisees, which is hypocrisy",*

He was categorically saying that their way of life is hypocrisy, and that like *leaven*, they can infect an entire congregation with their lifestyle of hypocrisy.

WHAT IS HYPOCRISY?

In ancient Greek drama or acting, there was only one individual with a set of masks depicting the characters he would be playing on stage. So, one by one, he picked up a mask, placed it over his face and proceeded to speak and act in a manner that would depict that character. When that character's role was over, he would then pick up another mask and likewise portray the character the mask represents. So, hypocrites were actors, or pretenders, as they were then called!

Hypocrites historically were, therefore, people who pretended to be characters they never intended to become. They only portrayed those characters to an audience; and afterwards, would return to their usual lifestyle.

So, when the Lord spoke of the *leaven* of the Pharisees being hypocrisy, He implied that what the Pharisees did and spoke openly was for a public audience, but their real character in private was different from who people saw in public! Thus, in **Matthew 23**, the Lord told the people,

> *"The teachers of the Law and the Pharisees are the authorised interpreters of Moses' Law. So you must obey and follow everything they tell you to do; do not, however, imitate their actions, because they don't practice what they preach. (**Matthew 23:2-3, GNB**)*

The Lord was essentially saying that when the Pharisees taught the Law of Moses, they were speaking what the Law says. However, when it came to practising what they had taught, they were unwilling and unable to live by what they taught the people.

Hypocrisy is thus, deception, duplicity, or dissimulation. It is pretending to be who you are not, nor intend to be. Hypocrisy is the opposite of integrity! Unlike hypocrites, people of integrity are wholesome. They have no parts that manifest differently in different situations. They are the same whether they are in public or in private. They say what they mean to say and do what they have said. In other words, they practice what they preach!

THE PROBLEM OF HYPOCRISY IN THE CHURCH

Hypocrisy is a problem in many homes because children learn more by what they see than by what they hear. So, when a parent engages in illegality and says to the child not to do the same, it is difficult for the child to obey because children find it easier to copy what they have seen than what they are being told.

The same is true of any leader-follower situation. People tend to follow what the leader does rather than what they say. A true leader is an example to their followers.

> *Shepherd the flock of God which is among you, serving as overseers, not by compulsion but willingly, not for dishonest gain but eagerly; nor as being lords over those entrusted to you, but being examples to the flock (**1 Peter 5:2-3**)*

During the early days of the COVID-19 pandemic, we saw some leaders who asked their citizens to mask up, but they did not do the same! They asked people to avoid crowded spaces, while they hosted large gatherings, for which some of them paid a heavy price!

We have the same problem in the church. Christians follow their pastors' lifestyle rather than what the pastors say from the pulpit! For this reason, hypocrisy is rife among those who work closely with hypocritical pastors. These associates of hypocritical pastors tend to act like God's word is not binding on them because their pastors act that way! They live recklessly and are carefree about observing God's word. These individuals live above the law of God because their principals act that way.

Hypocrisy is a lifestyle that many who claim to be Christians are living. They present a different face in a church meeting, another face at work, and yet a different personality at home! They can say a 'powerful prayer' filled with high sounding spiritual words, but their lives do not match what they pretend to be. These hypocrites are pious during church meetings and are thought of as saints by all. However, outside those gatherings, they are sexual predators, spouse abusers, bribe-takers, cult members, serial killers, occultic practitioners, etc.

Recent reports on some Christian leaders around the world leave a sour taste in the mouth. There have been accusations with overwhelming proof ranging from sexual predatory conduct, rape, gay lifestyle, spousal abuse, manipulations, deceptions, stealing, etc. Indeed, it is like observing **Galatians 5:19-21** play out in the church!

> *It is obvious what kind of life develops out of trying to get your own way all the time: repetitive, loveless, cheap sex; a stinking accumulation of mental and emotional garbage; frenzied and joyless grabs for happiness; trinket gods; magic-show religion; paranoid loneliness; cutthroat competition; all-consuming-yet-never-satisfied wants; a brutal temper; an impotence to love or be loved; divided homes and divided lives; small-minded and lopsided pursuits; the vicious habit of depersonalizing everyone into a rival; uncontrolled and uncontrollable addictions; ugly parodies of community. I could go on. This isn't the first time I have warned you, you know. If you use your freedom this way, you will not inherit God's kingdom. (**Galatians 5:19-21, MSG**)*

Living as described in the above passage of Scripture is evidence of living apart from the Holy Spirit's leading. The context of this passage of Scripture is **Galatians 5:16-18**:

> *My counsel is this: Live freely, animated and motivated by God's Spirit. Then you won't feed the compulsions of selfishness. For there is a root of sinful self-interest in us that is at odds with a free spirit, just as the free spirit is incompatible with selfishness. These two ways of life are antithetical, so that you cannot live at times one way and at times another way according to how you feel on any given day. Why don't you choose to be led by the Spirit and so escape the erratic compulsions of a law-dominated existence? (**Galatians 5:16-18, MSG**)*

So rampant is hypocrisy in the church of God, that it is safe to say that many of those attending church meetings are pretenders! They sing and play instruments in fellowship meetings on Sundays but also play in nightclubs on other days—sometimes, even coming to church meetings straight from the nightclubs! They are gentle brothers and sisters at fellowship meetings on Sundays, but rapists and seducers in their neighbourhoods and offices; they are benevolent in church but stingy in the wages they pay their employees and even with what they provide their families. They cannot hurt a fly in the glare of fellowship attendees but are involved in the most heinous crimes you can ever imagine: rape, armed robbery, murder, ritual killings, occultism, etc. The story of Dennis Rader[12], popularly known as the BTK (bind, torture, kill) murderer, comes to mind; he was a Sunday School teacher and the President of the Board of the church he attended, but he was a serial killer!

Indeed, the church of God on earth is experiencing an identity crisis. We no longer know, or at best are unsure of, who we are, what we are about, and where we will ultimately end up. To all intents and purposes, the line between the church and the world is all but nonexistent. We no longer can tell whether an individual is a Christian, even when they insist that they are. The *fruit of the Spirit* is not evident in many people who claim to be Christians, though they may speak in tongues! It makes one wonder what 'tongue' they are speaking—that of the Holy Spirit or some other spirit?

When Christians engage in acts that are clearly unscriptural and they are called out, rather than repent, they go all out to defend and espouse such acts as virtuous. This they do in a bid to legitimise a clearly illegitimate act or conduct.

THE ANTIDOTE TO A LIFE OF HYPOCRISY

If we must avoid the corruption of the *leaven-laden* lifestyle of some religious leaders' which is hypocrisy, we must return to God fully! We must repent of our hypocrisy, plead with God to strip us of all hypocrisy, and then build in us the true doctrine of Christ. The doctrine of Christ is not flamboyant but simple, yet with far-reaching positive impact in the lives of His adherents. We must live a life of integrity: our conduct must be the same for good in every situation and circumstance. A life of integrity cannot be lived in the flesh. It can only be truly possible with the divine nature. And to acquire the divine nature, we must get rid of the old nature of *leaven*.

This process is entirely a divine operation which can be achieved when we yield to the Holy Spirit.

> *Grace and peace be multiplied to you in the knowledge of God and of Jesus our Lord, as His divine power has given to us all things that pertain to life and godliness, through the knowledge of Him who called us by glory and virtue, by which have been given to us exceedingly great and pre-*

---

12   https://www.biography.com/crime-figure/dennis-rader

cious promises, that through these you may be partakers
of the divine nature, having escaped the corruption that is
in the world through lust. (2 Peter 1:2-4)

Let us be content to receive the incorruptible seed of God's word and stop seeking after contaminated messages of motivational speakers. These are high sounding words that only lead people into more sin. It cannot deliver those who adhere to it from the shackles of sin and sinful living.

Let us develop patience and self-control, among other spiritual attributes that cancel out and repel the old nature. This scriptural remedy eliminates the frustration, depression, and discontent we experience when things are not going our way. Paul said,

> *I am so happy, and I thank the Lord that you have again*
> *shown your care for me. You continued to care about me,*
> *but there was no way for you to show it. I am telling you*
> *this, but not because I need something. I have learned to*
> *be satisfied with what I have and with whatever happens.*
> *I know how to live when I am poor and when I have plen-*
> *ty. I have learned the secret of how to live through any*
> *kind of situation—when I have enough to eat or when I*
> *am hungry, when I have everything I need or when I have*
> *nothing. (Philippians 4:10-12, ERV)*

We need to understand that once you are born again, you belong to Christ. Therefore, you should be subject to Him in all things. You should yield to whatever He asks you to do and not do your own bidding.

> *Brethren, join in following my example, and note those*
> *who so walk, as you have us for a pattern. For many walk,*
> *of whom I have told you often, and now tell you even*
> *weeping, that they are the enemies of the cross of Christ:*
> *whose end is destruction, whose God is their belly, and*
> *whose glory is in their shame—who set their mind on*
> *earthly things. (Philippians 3:17-19)*

The Holy Spirit's purpose in the above Scripture verses is to warn Christians everywhere against following just anyone. He wants us to be mindful and to ensure that those we follow are indeed following Christ. In **1 Corinthians 11:1**, Paul again wrote,

> *Imitate me, just as I also imitate Christ. (1 Corinthians*
> *11:1)*

By this Scripture verse the Holy Spirit tells us that Christ is the standard! If you are following anyone, you had better be sure that they are following Christ! In his advice to pastors, Peter wrote,

> *Shepherd the flock of God which is among you, serving as overseers, not by compulsion but willingly, not for dishonest gain but eagerly; nor as being lords over those entrusted to you, but being examples to the flock (**1 Peter 5:2-3**)*

The pastor should be an example for the congregation to follow. If he is not to lead them into error, he must follow Christ! The pastor or spiritual leader must live a life of self-denial. The Lord said that for the sake of the disciples, He sanctified Himself (**John 17:19**) thus, setting an example for us to follow. The Lord warned that unless we deny ourselves of the lure of the world and die to self, we cannot be His disciples (**Luke 14:25-33**). Thus, when the congregants follow a righteous and godly leader, they are in effect following Christ!

There is also the obligation and responsibility of the congregation to follow Christ Himself! The leader is only an example. The leader is not Christ! We should only follow the leader in so far as the leader is following Christ. The church leader's lifestyle ought to inspire the church to live as Christ lived.

Before many congregants today, is the challenge to follow Christ, but many choose to follow people. Unfortunately, many of those people that other people follow are hypocrites masquerading as ministers of the gospel (**2 Corinthians 11:13-15**)! What then is the solution or antidote to the hypocrisy in the church? Follow Christ!

HOW DO I FOLLOW CHRIST?

Someone might say,

"Christ is not here for me to see and follow; so, how do I follow Him?"

The truth is, Christ is here by the Holy Spirit and through His word as contained in the Bible. Every time we read the Bible, we see what Christ is asking us to do, and we have the Holy Spirit to supply us with the enablement, so to do.

But to get to that place of seamless interaction between us and the Holy Spirit, we must be sanctified. Sanctification is what the Holy Spirit does in our lives once we are born again, so that we can obey God.

An unsanctified person is incapable of obeying God. Hence, the Holy Spirit comes to make the required changes in our lives so that we can obey God.

*For those who live according to the flesh set their minds on the things of the flesh, but those who live according to the Spirit, the things of the Spirit. For to be carnally minded is death, but to be spiritually minded is life and peace. Because the carnal mind is enmity against God; for it is not subject to the Law of God, nor indeed can be. So then, those who are in the flesh cannot please God. But you are not in the flesh but in the Spirit, if indeed the Spirit of God dwells in you. Now if anyone does not have the Spirit of Christ, he is not His. (**Romans 8:5-9**)*

The carnal man or mind is the nature or personality in anyone—male or female—that is unsanctified. The Holy Spirit is unable to and cannot lead such an individual. But why can't the Holy Spirit lead an unsanctified person? The Holy Spirit does not herd people; He shepherds them! He gently urges them but neither compels nor coerces them. Hence, God said,

*I will instruct you and teach you in the way you should go; I will guide you with My eye. Do not be like the horse or like the mule, Which have no understanding, Which must be harnessed with bit and bridle, Else they will not come near you. (**Psalms 32:8-9**)*

If you find it difficult, or are unwilling to obey God, then you have not permitted the Holy Spirit to sanctify you; you have in effect, shut your heart from the Holy Spirit. And with this, there can only be one consequence—a life of dissimulation. The unsanctified person wants to live as he or she wants but give the impression that they are living as Christ desires. Everything they do, like the Pharisees and the Scribes before them, they do for show (**Matthew 23:5; 6:1-6, 16**)!

Chapter 4

Sanctification

What is sanctification, and how potent is it against leaven?

WHAT IS SANCTIFICATION?

All that has been said about the antidote to hypocrisy points to sanctification as the panacea to the problem of *leaven* and hypocrisy. So, let us talk about it.

Sanctification is generally known as the second work of grace, which God does through the Holy Spirit in the life of one who has already received the grace of salvation through faith in Jesus Christ. Through Ezekiel, God reveals how sanctification works:

> *I will give you a new heart and put a new spirit within you; I will take the heart of stone out of your flesh and give you a heart of flesh. I will put My Spirit within you and cause you to walk in My statutes, and you will keep My judgments and do them. (Ezekiel 36:26-27)*

What the Holy Spirit does is to remove, not repair, the evil heart or the human nature that loves to sin in us and replace it with the nature of God! Human nature is corrupt, *ab initio*, and continues to deteriorate, growing more corrupt with each passing day. It cannot be repaired because it is evil through and through. The only thing to do is to remove and replace it.

This is spiritual 'surgery' that the Holy Spirit performs. And like normal surgery, where you have to give consent, you must give your consent to the Holy Spirit for Him to take away the unyielding heart and replace it with a heart that delights in doing the will of God alone!

SANCTIFICATION'S POTENCY AGAINST HYPOCRISY

It is important to note that sanctification results in 'a new heart', not a repaired old heart; but a brand new heart! Thus, the Bible says,

> *Therefore, if anyone is in Christ, he is a new creation; old things have passed away; behold, all things have become new. (**2 Corinthians 5:17**)*

Sanctification gives you a new nature, making you a new man—*a new creation*! With a new godly heart, you cannot be a hypocrite; neither can hypocrites deceive you because pleasing God alone will be your focus!

Indeed, when you become "a child of God", all things become new in the real sense of the phrase, and you become like Christ: a new personality with new plans, new purposes, new priorities—everything is new—all from God!

There is more. We are purged, purified, and prepared to render acceptable and holy service unto God through sanctification. Apart from sanctification you cannot serve God acceptably because you will be doing everything in the flesh, which is contaminated and corrupt. It is like someone serving you with a piece of bread with mould or fungus on it. If you were to cut off the visible infected part, you would then encounter a darker and more offensive mould on the inside because the piece of bread is truly contaminated by mould. You just would be unable to eat such a piece of bread.

In the same way, the unsanctified individual has 'mould' (sin) in every aspect of their life—their worship, prayer, preaching, Bible Study, everything! They are contaminated and repulsive to God. This contamination is the hypocrisy that makes the individual seem acceptable to people because they are doing what is religious. In reality, those things are acts that only an idol can accept!

Anything that God will accept must be sanctified and holy. Hence, the Lord Jesus prayed the Father regarding His disciples, of which we are, to:

> *Sanctify them by Your truth. Your word is truth.* (**John 17:17**)

The Easy-to-Read Version of the Bible infers the essence of sanctification thus:

> *Make them ready for your service through your truth. Your teaching is truth.* (**John 17:17, ERV**)

An unsanctified person is a hypocrite by nature and can only be healed of their hypocrisy through sanctification. Jesus' apostles manifested strange behaviour while Jesus was with them in person because they were not yet sanctified. And they were not sanctified at that time because Jesus had not yet gone to the cross nor resurrected! For instance, there was the time when James and John wanted Jesus to call down fire upon a village because they wouldn't allow them to stay there and preach (**Luke 9:51-56**). Another instance was Peter's denial of the Lord as variously recorded in the gospels.

The Holy Spirit lets us into this allusion of sanctification coming after the Lord's resurrection, when He tells us through John's gospel thus:

> *The last day of the festival came. It was the most important day. On that day Jesus stood up and said loudly, "Whoever is thirsty may come to me and drink. If anyone believes in me, rivers of living water will flow out from their heart. That is what the Scriptures say." Jesus was talking about the Spirit. The Spirit had not yet been given to people, because Jesus had not yet been raised to glory. But later, those who believed in Jesus would receive the Spirit.* (**John 7:37-39, ERV**)

But once they were sanctified after Jesus' resurrection, their behaviour changed. It must be stated at this juncture that sanctification is not a once-and-for-all affair. No! It is a process that must continue until we go home to be with the Lord in eternity.

For instance, do you wash your clothes once and never again? As long as you wear them, you must wash them regularly to keep them clean and useful to you.

In a well-furnished kitchen there are not only crystal goblets and silver platters, but waste cans and compost buckets—some containers used to serve fine meals, others to take out the garbage. Become the kind of container God can use to present any and every kind of gift to his guests for their blessing. Run away from infantile indulgence. Run after mature righteousness—faith, love, peace—joining those who are in honest and serious prayer before God. Refuse to get involved in inane discussions; they always end up in fights. God's servant must not be argumentative, but a gentle listener and a teacher who keeps cool, working firmly but patiently with those who refuse to obey. You never know how or when God might sober them up with a change of heart and a turning to the truth, enabling them to escape the Devil's trap, where they are caught and held captive, forced to run his errands. (2 Timothy 2:20-26, MSG)

Sanctification is, therefore, the means by which the Christian is purged of the old nature of sin and infused with the new nature of righteousness. Through sanctification, we fall in love with God, hate sin, and delight in God's word. It is impossible for the sanctified individual to willingly sin or try to cover up sin when it is brought to their notice by the Holy Spirit. Sanctification is thus the way to deal with hypocrisy in our lives.

Conclusion

The difference between the Christian who is living as God desires and those who live differently, is sanctification.

As we conclude, let us note that when people are not continually sanctified, they often relapse into a life of sin. This is when we say that they are *'backslidden'*! And to mask their backsliding, people live false lives and end up being hypocrites.

When we struggle to obey God, we are essentially still infected by the *leaven* of hypocrisy! To drive home this point, I present here, a satirical story of the grass-eating goat that was never able to stop eating grass!

GOATEE, THE GRASS-EATING GOAT, AND ITS OWNER

The story told below is an illustration of what real change looks like for the Christian. It illustrates what we must do if we are to experience real transformation in our lives.

LET US MEET GOATEE

There once was a goat, called Goatee, who loved to eat grass, as all goats do. Unfortunately, Goatee's owner, who had a luscious garden, understandably, did not share Goatee's passion for eating grass.

Goatee's quick thinking thwarted every attempt by its owner to ward it off his garden. For instance, when Goatee's owner built a hedge around the garden, Goatee ate its way through, and when he made a fence around it, Goatee head-butted its way in. Not knowing what else to do, Goatee's owner decided it needed counselling.

GOATEE GOES FOR COUNSELLING

So off to counselling, they went. The trained counsellor, a psychologist of repute, tried to get Goatee to think of other things besides its owner's luscious garden. The counsellor told Goatee to recite, "*My owner's garden is not food, but a work of art*" whenever the urge to eat grass came upon him, or at least a hundred times daily.

Following counselling, the owner had a respite from defending his garden until the day his neighbours came to his home with batons demanding that he surrender Goatee. It was then he realised that even though Goatee had let his garden be, it had gone to his neighbours' gardens instead. So, they returned to counselling. The counsellor, who was a Christian, then suggested that Goatee be taken to church for deliverance and become born again.

GOATEE GOES TO CHURCH

So, off to church, they went—Goatee and its owner. In church, before the service began, Goatee's owner told the pastor the difficulty he was having with Goatee. The pastor excitedly said that his sermon that morning incidentally was to be about change and advised Goatee to listen attentively and do whatever ministered to it. At this point, Goatee was getting stressed with everyone knowing his business and issues with grass. So, Goatee made up its mind to give this a try also.

During the service, the sermon, titled "*Changing your way of life*", stressed the fact that our actions affect other people and that unless we change our behaviour, we would soon find ourselves in big trouble, if not becoming isolated from everyone else. The pastor concluded by announcing that such a change is possible when we become born again through repentance.

The pastor then gave an "altar call"—an invitation to those who want to repent and be born again to come forward. Goatee's owner nudged Goatee forward. Goatee went to the altar and said the "sinner's prayer"—a prayer of confession of wrong done and acceptance of Jesus into its life—all the while wondering how grass-eating was sinful. Afterwards, the pastor gleefully told Goatee that it was now born again and a new creature. It was a day of joy and relief for both Goatee and its owner.

GOATEE IS BORN AGAIN!

Happily, they went home, announced to the neighbours that their gardens were now safe because "Goatee is now born again!" Goatee and its owner were now regulars at church services, and many of the neighbours who were not attending church services began going for church meetings. Goatee was no longer seen as a threat or an enemy and had free access to everyone's compound. Initially, the neighbours were apprehensive, but after a while, they felt safe, especially seeing that Goatee had become a worker in the church and had the most wonderful baritone in the church choir.

THE UNRAVELLING OF GOATEE

One day, one of the neighbours found a massive patch in his garden. Not wanting to believe Goatee's culpability and raise unwarranted suspicion nor offend Goatee's owner, she kept quiet about it. Unknown to her, other neighbours had had the same experience.

When the matter came to light, everyone was disappointed in Goatee, including the pastor and Goatee's choir colleagues. Goatee never really changed; it merely used its church attendance as a garb to ward off suspicion. The shame was too much to bear, so Goatee's owner sold off his property and together with Goatee, they relocated to another part of the world.

SO WHAT WENT WRONG WITH GOATEE?

Why was Goatee unable to stop its 'bad habit'? What really could have been done to help Goatee? These were questions that bothered the pastor. As he pondered these things, God said to him, "Answering an "altar call", saying the "sinner's prayer", being an active participant in church activities and even joining the church workforce or singing in the choir does not mean that a person has changed."

The Lord told him that bringing an individual to Christ through repentance was only the beginning of the journey. "That individual must go through changes in their lives by the Holy Spirit's working in them through the preaching and teaching of God's word." The Lord continued, "Being born again allows the Holy Spirit access into an individual's life so that meaningful change can take place. This change is radical; it changes everything about the personality since it changes the very essence of the person—their nature!"

The Lord explained further, "The natural man cannot but sin because of the sin-loving nature of all human beings, just as Goatee could not help eating grass! It is natural for goats to eat grass. You will need a spiritual surgical procedure to get a goat to stop eating grass. No matter the quantum of preaching, you cannot get the natural man to love God. Outwardly, they seem to love God, but they cannot obey Him. They struggle and cannot overcome sin. Even when they hate what they are doing, they cannot help themselves. Thus, the work of the Holy Spirit is first to change the nature of people from sin-loving to God-loving."

Then the pastor understood what the Lord meant when He told His disciples,

*"Those who love me will do what I say." (**John 14:23, GW**)*

He also realised that he had been trying to change people by merely preaching and thinking that those who told him that his sermons were great would change!

LAUNDERERS AND THEIR DETERGENT

Beloved, like Goatee in our fictitious story, we cannot stop our wrong behaviour by merely being born again, attending church meetings, and even becoming workers and ministers in the church. You need a combination of the Holy Spirit and God's word to change your sin-loving nature.

It is like a launderer and detergent. No matter how strong the launderer is, without detergent, the clothes would be bruised, damaged, and unclean still. On the other hand, merely soaking clothes in the detergent does not make clothes clean, and the longer the clothes remain soaked in the detergent-solution, the worse they would become—the fabric will be weakened and stained and may eventually develop a staying foul odour.

The washing action of the launderer is required to remove stains and give the clothes a clean sparkle. The Holy Spirit is the Launderer, and God's word is the detergent. Therefore, the Holy Spirit (the Launderer) without God's word (the detergent) is a misnomer, and God's word without the Holy Spirit is abnormal! Through God's word, the Holy Spirit works to bring about permanent positive change in an individual who is born again.

MERELY DESIRING CHANGE IS NOT ENOUGH TO CAUSE A CHANGE!

Many of us would love to see changes in our lives and in the lives of others, but merely desiring change does not translate to a change! The desire for change is good, but why do you want it?

Goatee desired change because of the misery it was bringing to its owner and the associated stress. Goatee's owner and their neighbours wanted Goatee to change to safeguard their gardens. The pastor desired change for Goatee because it increased church attendance.

THE HYPOCRISY OF MODERN CHRISTIANITY

The moment Goatee's behaviour no longer grieved people around it, Goatee relapsed but learnt to cover up its wrong acts! Today, many hypocrites shuffle in and out of church buildings and meetings. These *'Christians'* have perfected the art of covering up their sins.

They are even so bold as to justify the sins of others. They would not confess their sins before God nor seek His help. Unfortunately, we may justify our sins before men, but not before God, Who sees and knows the intent of all men!

CHANGING OUR NATURE

God desires to change our sin-loving human nature to a God-loving divine nature. Getting us there is a process that is aptly captured in **2 Peter 1.**

> *His [**God's**][13] divine power has given to us all things that pertain to life and godliness, through the knowledge of Him who called us by glory and virtue, by which have been given to us exceedingly great and precious promises, that through these you may be partakers of the divine nature, having escaped the corruption that is in the world through lust. But also for this very reason, giving all diligence, add to your faith virtue, to virtue knowledge, to knowledge self-control, to self-control perseverance, to perseverance godliness, to godliness brotherly kindness, and to brotherly kindness love. For if these things are yours and abound, you will be neither barren nor unfruitful in the knowledge of our Lord Jesus Christ. For he who lacks these things is shortsighted, even to blindness, and has forgotten that he was cleansed from his old sins. Therefore, brethren, be even more diligent to make your call and election sure, for if you do these things you will never stumble (**2 Peter 1:3-10**)*

Being born again is like being born into a home. Yes, you are now a member of the family. Still, you will need to be nurtured to maturity and become a responsible member of the family, exhibiting the family's nature or traits.

To exhibit the nature of God, the Scripture passage above tells us that we must grow from faith at salvation, to displaying moral excellence or integrity; that is, living right by God's standard. Then, we must learn more about God, not just for knowledge's sake, but to know Him intimately and then allow Him to control us; this is what is referred to as self-control. No one can control himself or

---

13   Author's infusion

herself, but we can yield to the Holy Spirit's control. The Holy Spirit's control then leads to perseverance which is the trait of enduring things unpalatable to the sin-loving human nature, like hardship, a desire for vengeance, inability to wait for something to happen in its time, suffering deprivation without resentment, etc.

Perseverance then manifests in godliness; that is, living a godly life; a God-pleasing life. Godliness manifests in brotherly kindness, which then culminates in having love for all human beings, regardless of their skin colour, nationality, tribe, ethnicity, economic status, political affiliation, religious beliefs, etc. Such a spiritual growth process does not breed hypocrisy but makes us understand the achievable goal that God has set before us.

Not growing this way is a sure sign that we are stunted in our Christian development. Indeed, Peter describes this as shortsightedness, if not blindness, regarding the change that occurred at salvation. Such short-sightedness often leads people to relapse, or backslide, to the old lifestyle of sin and sinful pleasures.

GOATEE'S RELAPSE MANIFESTS AS THE CHRISTIAN'S HYPOCRITICAL LIFESTYLE

Today, we read about renowned '*Christian leaders*' worldwide who lived, or, are living hypocritical lifestyles. These '*Christian leaders*' have mastered the art of living a double life; it is natural to them. Far worse is the impact of their hypocritical lifestyle on other Christians, especially on those most influenced by their teachings.

And herein is another protection which God has given us: He does not want us to venerate (or exalt) servants of God but His word, which is unfailing! Human beings may fail or fall, but God's word neither fails nor falls. You can trust it!

GOD'S DESIRE IS "NO MORE RELAPSE!"

God's desire has always been that all who come to Him will eternally be with Him. To achieve this, He takes responsibility for changing our nature from a sin-loving nature to a God-loving nature. In the state of a God-loving nature, we will effortlessly live for God and avoid and repudiate sin. And this, beloved, is what a changed life is all about!

One caveat is that you must be willing to make yourself available to God to make the necessary changes!

TAKE HEED AND BEWARE

For those discerning and heaven-conscious individuals, the Lord's remark about *leaven* is a crucial statement of caution. Doctrines and teachings from people who seem religious can subvert, and have indeed, subverted whole congregations and peoples groups, the world over!

Unleavened bread is dense and tough to tear and chew, but only a little of it is satisfying; so is the doctrine of Christ. In the absence of *leaven*, the doctrine of Christ seems uninteresting, but it is the bread of life! Once you introduce 'the *leaven* of false doctrine' into Christian living, it becomes the bread of lies, leading to death! It may be dainty to the palate, it may sound good, but it definitely leads to death!

Therefore, '*take heed and beware*' of the *leaven* of the Pharisees, the Sadducees, and of the Herodians. That means, take heed and beware of the doctrines, teachings, philosophies, ideologies, principles, and manner of living, etc. of religious and political leaders! The masquerading of hypocritical religious leaders and their counterpart politicians as God's servants is very much alive and in our midst today—Beware!

BEWARE OF HYPOCRISY

The Lord did not just warn us to beware of the hypocrisy (and double-standards) of church leaders; He also implied that we should not get infected with it! If you find that you are unwilling to obey God or are struggling to do so, then, you need to pray to God to send the Holy Spirit to sanctify you because that is how you will be able to live a life of integrity.

Being saved or born again only makes it possible for the Holy Spirit to come into your heart and do His work therein. Without being born again, an individual born on earth is contaminated from birth because of the sin of Adam and Eve, which was rebellion and disobedience to God. Everyone born of a man and woman is a hypocrite from birth for this reason. We may look innocent but are very capable of committing the most heinous crimes. When we get born again, the capacity to sin is still present in our lives, but it is sanctification by the Holy Spirit that deals decisively with the issue of sin. Thus, being born again does not automatically deal with sin—sanctification does, and it is a continuous daily process until the day we fall asleep in the Lord.